Machine Learning in Cyber Security

Network Traffic Classification based on Class Weight-based K-NN Classifier (CWK-NN)

Mohamad Osama Hijazi

Jawad Khalife

ELIVA PRESS

ELIVA PRESS

Mohamad Osama Hijazi

Jawad Khalife

This book is addressed for both seasoned and beginners in the field of machine learning, we included a simple explanation for each idea and then we expanded to all technical details. We started by explaining KNN and all its challenges. Then we introduced a newly discovered dataset deficiency and an enhancement to counter that problem. The field of the experiment was on network traffic classification. We combined the precision of the DPI method and the privacy of blind classifiers, once the model is trained on known traffic flows, then we used the statistical data and the packet header for classification.

Published by Eliva Press SRL
Address: MD-2060, bd.Cuza-Voda, 1/4, of. 21 Chişinău, Republica
Moldova
Email: info@elivapress.com
Website: www.elivapress.com

ISBN: 978-1-63648-076-3

Network Traffic Classification based on

Class Weight based K-NN Classifier (CWK-NN)

Mohamad Hijazi

School of Arts and Sciences

Lebanese International University

Nabatieh, Lebanon

MohamadOsamaHijazi@Gmail.com

Jawad Khalife

School of Arts and Sciences

Lebanese International University

Beirut, Lebanon

jkhalife.khalife@liu.edu.lb

ABSTRACT

Identifying network applications is centric to nowadays' networks, both from network management and security standpoints. Port-based classification is obsolete and researchers are seeking new methods to classify traffic by inspecting other fields in IP packet header and payload. Consequently, a large number of approaches exist in the literature, some are based on deep packet inspection, which discloses the packet payload and raises privacy concerns, while others rely on discriminative traffic attributes at the network and transport layers, such as packet sizes and inter-arrival times. Machine learning techniques have been widely used in the literature, especially the K Nearest Neighbor due to its simplicity, zero-time for training, and adequacy for general classification contexts. However, a major drawback of KNN is its dependency on the training set, being a lazy classification algorithm with no classification model to build. In this work, we aim first at assessing KNN algorithm in traffic classification contexts through an experimental test-bed that we build for this purpose. Second, we explore new challenges related KNN training datasets since they are the actual "model" on which KNN classification decision is made. While common known dataset deficiencies include outliers or imbalanced dataset problems, we explore and quantify a new deficiency, related to the training samples distribution in the n-dimensional space and class clusters' intersections. Then, instead of weighting training samples individually, as most literature works do, we weight classes based on distribution of the training samples and the intersections of class clusters found in the dataset. Finally, we propose a new Class Weight based KNN Classifier (CWKNN), an enhanced KNN algorithm that can easily adapt to the newly explored training set deficiency by using the class weighting scheme we defined. Our tests on real captured traffic, together with publically available datasets showed promising results (up to 7% enhancement in True Positives) especially when compared to the native and "weighted Samples" KNN approaches most often described in the literature.

1

Contents

1.Introduction

The ability to identify network applications is centric to many network management and security tasks, including quality of service assignment, traffic engineering, content-dependent pricing, resource allocation, traffic shaping, and others. With the proliferation of applications, many of them using different kinds of obfuscation, traditional port-based classification has long become obsolete.

Numerous methods were proposed for traffic classification (J. Khalife, A multilevel taxonomy and requirements for an optimal traffic-classification model, 2014)in the last decade. These methods have different characteristics at many levels, including the analyzed input, the applied techniques, and the classified target objects. Deciding upon which classification features to use is a strategic choice for any traffic classifier. Ideally, Deep packet inspection (digitalguardian, 2019) (J. Khalife, On the Performance of OpenDPI in Identifying P2P Truncated traffic, 2013), or DPI, evaluates the data part and the header of a packet that is transmitted through an inspection point. DPI goes beyond examining IP packet headers, therefore, it raises many privacy concerns and is not applicable when the traffic needing to be monitored is encrypted or tunneled. However, DPI techniques are considered in the literature as the most accurate techniques and are used therefore as reference classifiers to build the Ground Truth or reference results.

On the other hand, blind classifiers do not inspect the payload and have the potential ability to deal with these obstacles, at the expense of an acceptable sacrifice in accuracy. Though less accurate, the so called blind methods are preferred in most environments because they guarantee the users' privacy, have the potential to classify encrypted communications and usually require less computational power.

Most of these techniques are based on traffic attributes at the network and transport layers, such as packet sizes and inter-arrival times. Due to the problem dimensionality, Machine Learning (ML) techniques can be used in the classification context. ML classification is considered an instance of supervised learning, i.e., learning where a training set of correctly identified observations is available. An algorithm that implements classification, especially in a concrete implementation, is known as a classifier. In machine learning, the observations are often known as instances, the explanatory variables are termed features (grouped into a feature vector), and the possible categories to be predicted are classes. The term "classifier" sometimes also refers to the mathematical function, implemented by a classification algorithm that maps input data (traffic attributes in the traffic classification case) to a category (Application type like HTTP, NTP, DNS…etc.).

There is a relevant research activity in network traffic classification, employing different Machine learning approaches. Among them, KNN (Min Zhang, 2017) (Hou Kaihu, 2018) (Shweta Taneja,

2014) (Kumar, 2018) was used in several papers due to its simplicity and zero-training time, as will be shown in the next sections.

KNN (K Nearest Neighbor) algorithm was first proposed by Cover and Hart in 1968. The algorithm itself is simple and effective, which is a typical lazy or instance-based learning algorithm. It is not essential for the classifier to use the training set to train and the training time complexity is 0. With KNN, the function is only approximated locally and all computation is deferred until classification. The principle of K nearest neighbor classification algorithm (K-neighborhood) is that if the K samples in the eigenvalue space most closed to the sample to be identified almost belong to the same class, we determine this sample also belongs to such a class. The key difference between classification and regression tree (machinelearningmastery, 2018) is that in classification, the task is predicting a discrete class label while in regression, the task consists of predicting a continuous quantity.

1.1. Background of the Work

Despite of the stated advantages and simplicity, a major drawback of KNN, as previously mentioned, is its dependency on the training set. In fact, one of the most important aspects of KNN is being a lazy ML algorithm in the sense that it does not build a model based on the training dataset. Rather, every time we need to classify a record, we should first have a samples set and to perform the distance calculation between all the instances. KNN is a lazy classification algorithm that does not build a classification model based on the labeled instances in the training dataset. As such, a relevant question can be raised at this level:

Is it possible to evaluate the validity of KNN training sets? Could the classes inside each training set be weighted according to some more advanced characteristics as to evaluate their credibility in training KNN classifiers? Moreover, could KNN classifier adapt to existing deficiencies discovered in the training dataset as to maintain or enhance the classification accuracy?

In this research, we attempt to answer these questions in the computer network traffic classification context, and we seek to explore and weight newly explored deficiencies in KNN training sets while deriving a new customized KNN approach.

1.2. Originality and Contribution

In this journal, we study and explore new deficiencies in the KNN training datasets, independently from the relative number of the training samples' (known as imbalance problem in the literature), but

4

related to their distribution and level of spread in the n-dimensional space (n being the number of attributes).

For this reason, we cluster classes and measure their intersections in the training set and weight corresponding classes accordingly, instead of weighting or sampling training points individually, as most of the literature works do.

Then, we propose a new Class Weight based KNN Classifier (CWKNN) that is able of considering the new class weights.

Finally, we compare results to the native or weighted samples KNN approaches found in the literature. Throughout our experiments, we also aim at assessing KNN algorithm in general traffic classification contexts based on an experimental test-bed we build for this purpose and across several datasets.

1.3. Methodology

To test existing and newly proposed approaches, we proceeded as follows:

First, we built an experimental setup where we capture, parametrize (attributes extraction) and classify (or label) real computer traffic using reference classification tools found in the literature, in order to obtain the ground truth results (reference results used for evaluation.

Then, using this labelled data, together with our classification platform we used for this purpose, we apply non-labelled attribute vectors extracted previously, to the classifiers relevant for our work for evaluation purposes. We start first by evaluating KNN and weighted Samples KNN approaches (as will be detailed later in this journal) and our newly proposed CWKNN approach.

Finally, we compare the results with the ground truth as to evaluate existing vs. newly proposed classifiers.

1.4. Jouranl Overview

The structure of this journal is as follows: Chapter 2 presents the related work and recent KNN related papers in computer traffic classification, while explaining the native algorithm and highlighting on key related challenges; Chapter 4 details how we explore a new deficiency for KNN training set and how we derive a new KNN approach that weights and considers the newly explored deficiency;chapter 3 includes the native KNN explanation, and the limitations it face ;Chapter 4 presents the experimental setup and traffic datasets through which existing and proposed classifiers

5

were evaluated; Chapter 5 presents the experimental results and finally, Chapter 6 presents the conclusions and future work.

Chapter 2: Literature Review

A large number of traffic classification approaches exist in the literature, some are based on deep packet inspection, which discloses the packet payload and raises privacy concerns, while others rely on discriminative traffic attributes at the network and transport layers, such as packet sizes and inter-arrival times. This emergent research needs to arise since IANA Port-based classification (IANA, 2013) has become obsolete for more than one decade. Machine learning techniques have been widely used in the literature, especially the K Nearest Neighbor due to its simplicity, zero-time for training, and adequacy for general classification contexts.

Many papers in the literature used KNN for traffic classification and attempted to enhance the native algorithm by addressing key challenges. For example, to select the most appropriate K value for KNN, authors in (Kumar, 2018) used Dynamic KNN, distance weighted KNN, clustering the results, and building a model. Dynamic KNN is responsible for selecting the most appropriate K value for each dataset. In the training phase, K value is selected as well as calculating the weight of each sample, then having clusters in order to build a model. In the test phase, they calculate the distance between the center of each cluster and the test point X to be classified. After finding the nearest cluster, the weighted distance between X and the rest of the cluster samples is calculated. After determining the class of X they add it to the training dataset after calculating its weight. As a result, they preserved the same accuracy but were able to decrease the time to classify an instance by 50%. Authors in (TM, 2018) used fuzzy knn to enhance accuracy f score and g mean of pulsar selection algorithm. They a special weighting algorithm in the training phase, where they compute the relationship between the features and the class membership. Nearest neighbors are given high membership value to the class they are near from. However, the samples that are far from a class will be given a small membership value to this class. The proposed algorithm outperforms other machine learning algorithms in accuracy metric values starting from 0.01 to 0.04, G means metric from 0.03 to 0.06, and decreased the FPR value by 0.04 .

In (Lei Dinga), authors reduced the flow attributes used in classification by introducing a relationship between flows in order to derive an expanding vector of flow which represents the attributes of the classes. Their algorithm outperforms naïve base classifier with 3.2% of decrease in error rate and achieved 99% of accuracy.

Known DPI methods were enhanced in (Alok Tongaonkarﬂ, 2014) by introducing a methodology that automatically learns signatures for application. Their method enhances known DPI by identifying

7

new applications that old dpi cannot identify, has higher accuracy, handles variation in applications and adapts to changing network traffic without user intervention.

For making KNN cost sensitive, authors in (Zhang, 2019) applied smoothing, setting K with minimum cost, CS feature selection, and CS stacking. They also used instances weighting. They outperformed old KNN with performance increase ranging from 0.01 to 0.02 of average misclassification cost.

Other papers (Jigang Wang, 2006) focused on enhancing the distance measurement method. In (Jigang Wang, 2006) the authors introduced a new variable to the distance rule that made it dynamic. This variable represents the radius of a sphere centered on the new object and excluding all samples that have a distinct label, the distance between an unknown point X (to be classified) and samples that have the same "nature" is less than 1 while the distance between X and the different elements is 1. They tested the new algorithm on five different Datasets and values of K ranging from 1 to 50, with Manhattan, Euclidean distance methods used, they achieved lowering error rates up to 6%.

To enhance KNN by weight training samples, authors in (Kumar, 2018) used the sigmoid function and were able to decrease the error rate which ranged from 0.007 to 0.025 for 10 different datasets. Similarly, together with an improved distance method measure, authors in (Kumar, 2018) used entropy to weight the training samples contribution in the classification process. They achieved 3% of increased accuracy compared to native KNN over 4 tested datasets.

At a more granular level, authors in (Kumar, 2018) weight KNN attributes instead of samples. They applied a genetic algorithm to keep changing the weight of each attribute according to its contribution in the classification process. Then, weighted voting between neighbors is used instead of default KNN voting. For testing, they used a private (Kumar, 2018) and were able to reach accuracy enhancements between 1% and 3%. Similarly, weighting attributes for each sample was addressed in (machinelearningmastery, 2018), where authors applied entropy weight on each attribute, involving it in the distance calculation between neighbors. They tested the algorithm on 3 datasets using multiple K values and achieved enhancements ranging between 0.0118% and 0.0775%.

On the other hand, and to the best of our knowledge, no papers were found in the literature weighting the classes in the datasets or evaluating the validity of the training set itself for KNN classification.

Most importantly, KNN enhancements should address the dataset convenience for KNN classification. This is due to an intrinsic feature related to KNN, which is its strong dependency on the training set, being a lazy algorithm, as will be detailed later. Deficiencies in the datasets are amongst the most considerable KNN drawbacks when it comes to classification since KNN does not build a classification model, the training dataset itself is the built-in "model". Deficiencies in the KNN training datasets include imbalanced classes, outliers and other deficiencies that we will explain and quantify later in this work.

8

To the best of our knowledge, no papers were found in the literature weighting the classes in the datasets based on the training samples distribution in the n-dimensional space or independently from the imbalanced classes' problem. The most relevant paper is (pseudo_teetotaler, 2019) (Liu W., 2011).

In (pseudo_teetotaler, 2019), authors introduced a new method to calculate the validity rating and coherence of each label increasing the ability to set the class of the new member to the lowest occurrence class. They applied the algorithm on one dataset and multiple K values ranged from 1 to 20 and achieved an overall enhancement reaching 0.03 in the peek.

In (Liu W., 2011), authors propose CCW (class confidence weights) that uses the probability of attribute values given class labels to weight prototypes in KNN. Their main focus was, however, on the imbalanced classes' problem and they referred to sampling the training set.

In this journal, as mentioned previously, we tackle unexplored training set deficiencies based on their distribution of the training points in the n-dimensional space and class clusters mutual intersections. To measure the new dataset deficiency, we weight the class instead of the training samples, without sampling or neglecting any part of the training dataset. Then, through a new proposed KNN classifier, we aim at weighting the classes accordingly to analyze the impact of the newly explored "training set deficiency" on KNN classification and enhancing, at the same time, the native KNN approach by accommodating it to consider this newly explored deficiency in the training set. Experiments we conduct at last aim at assessing KNN for the traffic datasets we have besides comparing the different existing and newly proposed approach.

To achieve these goals, we had to understand the newly explored KNN training set deficiency with the associated KNN proposed approach that measures and accounts for this deficiency during classification, as shown next.

Chapter 3: The Native KNN Approach

KNN or K nearest neighbor algorithm is very simple algorithm yet very efficient. KNN starts by locating the k nearest neighbors for an unknown instance where K is a real number assigned by the user. After locating the neighbors of the object, a major voting takes place. The nature of the unknown object will be the class that got the highest number of votes in the neighboring area selected.

The nearest neighbors are determined by calculating the distance between the unknown instance and all the instances of the dataset.

As mentioned previously KNN Is a classification algorithm, It classifies objects based on the closest samples in the model that is composed of the whole or a subset of the training samples in the feature space. Thus, the classification consist of assigning the class of the K-nearest samples in the model to the input profile. The output is a y membership. An object is classified by a plurality vote of its neighbors, with the object being assigned to the y most common among its K nearest neighbors. In the classification phase, K is a user-defined constant, and an unknown object (H) is classified based on its attributes vector $(\vec{V}x)$ by assigning the label of the nearest neighbor (for K = 1), or through a majority voting process among the K nearest neighboring samples (for K > 1).

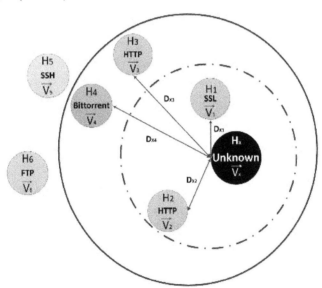

Figure 3.1: Native KNN classification

10

Hence, K is a critical parameter affecting the classification decision. As an example, Figure 3.1 shows some labeled samples, H1 to H4 and an unknown point, Hx. If K = 1, then the object is simply assigned to the class of that single nearest neighbor (SSL in this case, as per the closest host label, H1). However, it will be classified as HTTP for K = 4, as two of the four closest samples are labeled HTTP.

Annex-I depicts in pseudo-code how the native KNN classification, in classification or voting mode, is usually performed. It is obvious throughout KNN pseudo-code that the value of K is critical for KNN classification accuracy and computational overhead. It is also clear that KNN relies heavily on the training set characteristics to derive its classification decision, as described in this section.

1. KNN Classification Challenges

There exist no optimal classification algorithm (J. Khalife, A multilevel taxonomy and requirements for an optimal traffic-classification model, 2014) for all classification contexts. The performance of any machine learning classification algorithm is linked to two main factors, the algorithm itself and the data provided for training. Thereby, any deficiency in the classification is due either to the algorithm parameters which need to be fine-tuned and/or to the training phase process prior to classification.

In this work, though we focus more on the dataset deficiencies, we skim over known challenges related to KNN classification before addressing the training phase. KNN the algorithm has three main factors to be optimized for each application.

K value
As mentioned previously, the K value has a major impact in determining the nature of the instance to be classified, selecting a small value of K means that noise will have a higher influence on the result and a large value make it computationally expensive (pseudo_teetotaler, 2019). The only way to validate a KNN model (pseudo_teetotaler, 2019) is by the error on test data. In this work, we will fine-tune K as per the datasets we have, as will be shown in Section 5.

Distance type
The distance function plays a major role in KNN classification accuracy. Researches constantly enhance distance functions and add a new attribute to increase accuracy. To determine the proximity of two objects in the feature space, many distance types (Euclidean, Manhattan, Minkowski, etc.) may be used. Most relevant to our search are below:

1. Euclidean distance:

It's the straight line between point A and point B in a Euclidean space. The Euclidean distance between two n-dimensional points $\overrightarrow{Va} = [a1, a2 \ldots an]$ and $\overrightarrow{V_b}$ = [b1, b2, .., bn] is calculated as per the below equation:

Equation 0.1: Euclidean Distance

$$d(\overrightarrow{V_a}, \overrightarrow{V_b}) = \sqrt{\sum_{i=1}^{n} (b_i - a_i)^2}$$

2. **Minkowski:**

The Minkowski distance is a metric in a normed vector space which can be considered as a generalization of both the Euclidean distance and the Manhattan distance. The Minkowski distance of order p between points $\overrightarrow{Va}$ and $\overrightarrow{V_b}$ is defined as:

Equation 0.2: Minkowski Distance

$$d(\overrightarrow{V_a}, \overrightarrow{V_b}) = [\sum_{i=1}^{n} (b_i - a_i)^p]^{1/p}$$

Minkowski distance is typically used with p being 1 or 2, which correspond to the Manhattan distance and the Euclidean distance.

3. Mahalanobis distance:

The Mahalanobis distance is a measure of the distance between a point P and a distribution D, It is a multi-dimensional generalization of the idea of measuring how many standard deviations away P is from the mean of D. This distance is zero if P is at the mean of D, and grows as P moves away from the mean along each principal component axis. (contributors, 2020)

for further information check (whuber, 2020)

Equation 0.3: Mahalanobis Distance

$$d(M, \vec{x}) = \sqrt{(\vec{x} - \vec{\mu})^T s^{-1} (\vec{x} - \vec{\mu})}$$

Where s is the covariance matrix wich can be reduced to the Euclidean distance.

Weighting instances

One of the limitations for the traditional KNN is that it treats all the records (or training samples) of the training dataset in the same way. Practically, however, not all the records resemble its class perfectly as many records may have some of its characteristics far from the class average value. This process will decrease the accuracy of the classifier. Having one or 2 imperfect records in the voting process results in a wrong classified instance. The value of participation in taking decision denoted by weighting instances is very important since not all the records perfectly resemble the class they belong to, some records may be closer to a different class.

In consequence, it is fair to consider that some records decrease the accuracy and to be considered as noise yet other records perfectly resembles their class. As such, the process of weighting records is the approach of increasing the contribution of the unbiased records and decrease the contribution of the bad records.

2. Dataset deficiencies

As KNN classification decisions strongly depend on the training dataset, it is important to analyse the characteristics of the training data that may lead to any drawback in the classification process. These characteristics will be considered as deficiencies and include the below:

High unused dimensionality

For high-dimensional data (e.g., with number of dimensions more than 10) dimension reduction is usually performed prior to applying the k-NN algorithm in order to avoid the effects of the curse of dimensionality **Invalid source specified.**.

When the input data to an algorithm is too large to be processed and it is suspected to be redundant, then the input data will be transformed into a reduced representation set of features, through a process called feature extraction. Feature extraction is performed on raw data prior to applying k-NN algorithm on the transformed data in feature space.

Instances Outliers

An outlier is a data point that differs significantly from other observations. An outlier may be due to variability in the measurement or it may indicate the experimental error; the latter are sometimes excluded from the data set. Outliers, when found in the training dataset, can decrease the classification accuracy of KNN voting.

Finding such exception has received much attention in the data mining field. For example, one of the solutions **Invalid source specified.** is to partition the dataset into several clusters and then in each cluster, to calculates the Kth nearest neighborhood for the object to find outliers.

Class imbalance

A drawback of the basic "majority voting" classification occurs when the class distribution is skewed. That is, examples of a more frequent class tend to dominate the prediction of the new example because they tend to be common among the k nearest neighbors due to their large number.

One way to overcome this problem is to weight the classification, taking into account the distance from the test point to each of its k nearest neighbors. The class (or value, in regression problems) of each of the k nearest points is multiplied by a weight proportional to the inverse of the distance from that point to the test point.

Another way to overcome skew is by abstraction in data representation. For example, in a self-organizing map (SOM), each node is a representative (a center) of a cluster of similar points, regardless of their density in the original training data. K-NN can then be applied to the SOM.

In this work, problem dimensionality and features extraction are only assessed for the datasets we have. As stated earlier, we rather focus on quantifying key features in KNN training dataset, in order to be able to weight the dataset's classes accordingly. Having the classification accuracy in mind, a new proposed Class Weight based KNN Classifier (CWKNN) will be then derived accommodating to this new dataset-weighting scheme.

Chapter 4: Experimental Design

One of the objectives of this work, as previously stated, is to assess and to enhance KNN in traffic classification contexts. The completion of these objectives requires the accomplishment of some additional objectives related to building the experimental setup.

The target of the experimental setup is two-fold. First, it will be used to obtain the datasets of real traffic (data acquisition), and the associated Ground Truth (reference results) to be used for evaluating classification methods. Second, it will be used to extract a large set of traffic parameters that are potentially relevant for blind classification methods and that will be considered as the inputs for the traffic classification methods. Furthermore, the evaluation of the performance of the new proposal requires some metrics that will be introduced at the end of this section.

1.1 Classifier Reference Data

1.1.1 Main Experimental Steps
To build the ground-truth or reference results, three main steps (Figure 4.1) are needed:

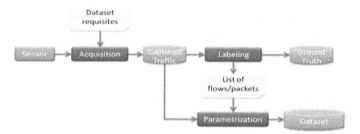

Figure 4.1: Acquisition, labeling and p parametrization of real traffic for experimental purposes.

1) Traffic Capture

First, a definition of a method and scenario for capturing real network traffic is required. The properties of this traffic are relevant from the point of view of the significance of the results and to enable having a reference set of labeled traffic (i.e. Ground Truth). For this, TCPDUMP **Invalid source specified.** , a well-known and widely used powerful command-line packet analyzer and sniffing tool, is used to capture the traffic from the network including:

- **Network and transport** layer headers
- **Full payload**, at least for a part the data to enable the use of DPI-based methods.

15

It is worthy to mention here that for some experiments, and to avoid any dataset bias, we used pre-processed datasets as found on the Internet, as will be shown later in this section.

2) Labeling and Classification:

Once the traffic is captured, it is necessary to classify it or a part of it with an accurate enough method as to be able to compare the results of the proposed methods. This labeled dataset will be the Ground Truth. For this, DPI (apache, ntop, 2019) will be used to assign a class to each packet/flow in the captured traces. Additionally, during the classification process, the existing flows and their associated packets will be identified and listed. The output of this step will be a list of flows with its assigned protocol, i.e. the ground truth, and the sets of packets in each flow.

3) Parametrization:

Third, each flow in the traffic is parameterized using a special tool according. The flows are parameterized through a vector of multiple characteristics or parameters, which will be described later in this section.

The appropriate implementation of the previous steps requires handling different formats for the data and the use of pre-developed and customized tools.

As depicted in Figure 3, this whole network is connected to the internet through an Internet Service Provider (ISP) using a single link. In this network, the optimal placement of the sensor to monitor and capture the traffic is at the main site between the WAN router and the firewall, as shown in Figure 4.2. This way, the sensor is able to observe the whole traffic from the inner nodes to both the Internet and the local servers before any NAT or proxy is applied. Therefore, full flows in both directions reaching any of the inner nodes can be observed. The sensor used is a PC-like host (monitoring host in Figure 3) configured with TCPDUMP.

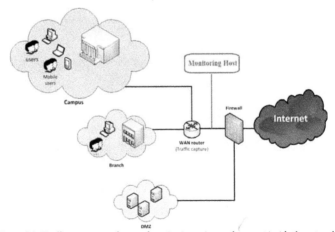

Figure 0.1: Traffic capture topology and monitoring point emplacement inside the network

16

1.1.2 Reference Classification Tool

The trace we used, referred to as capture sets (CS) was collected in the selected scenario during the capture process, over an extended period of time spanning around 3 days and totaling around 1.2 GB of real traffic.

The 3 days span of collecting the data was due to our desire to collect a large dataset for testing and classification and then we were obliged to use a part of the data collected for the lack of resources. And Knn classification algorithm stores all training dataset in the in the RAM.

In order to identify the existing flows in the captured dataset, that is, to obtain a list containing all the flows, we used nDPI (apache, ntop, 2019). As previously mentioned, this procedure is adopted under the assumption that DPI, by the time of this writing, is the most accurate traffic classification method with the minimum possible number of errors.

nDPI is a ntop-maintained superset of the popular OpenDPI library. The software is distributed under the GNU LGPLv3 license and available in source code format. nDPI can be used for the classification of flows and packets according to DPI-based methods. To the best of our knowledge, nDPI is the best currently available Open Source tool for traffic classification. nDPI can recognize up to 101 protocols.

1.1.3 Ground Truth Reference Results
Following the global procedure for the acquisition of the final datasets (Figure 4.3), the classification tool was used over the set of preprocessed files as generated in the first phase to obtaining the lists of labeled flows, i.e., the Ground Truth, and the lists of packets in each flow.

The results obtained for the aforementioned CS dataset are presented in Figure 4 and Table 1 where protocol distributions, in terms of the number and percentages of detected flows, are shown.

It is important to note that unknown traffic, i.e. unlabeled flows, was observed in each capture. Its relative high percentage cannot be attributed to a deficiency in the data capture itself, but rather, to the limitations of the classification tool. The fact is that, as previously stated, the native OpenDPI tool from which the tool is derived was unable to classify all the flows with its current library of application signatures and inspection methods. From a research point of view, the presence of unknowns is problematic since validation results should be 100% accurate. To handle this situation, unlabeled flows were omitted from the evaluation process.

Class	# Flows	Percentage
DNS	18492	35.73
ICMP	1191	2.30
HTTP	27154	52.47
MAIL_SMTP	1606	3.10
SNMP	3161	6.11
NTP	133	0.26
SIP	15	0.03
total	51752	100

Table 0.1: Protocol distribution for the CS dataset, (nDPI Ground Truth)

Obviously, the results show a different number of present protocols per dataset (imbalanced dataset). HTTP and DNS were the most predominant protocols which are expected in a real network environment where most applications and network services are web-based.

As for the unknown flows (e.g. 18.3% in CS) belong to encrypted applications using TCP ports 22, 80, and 443. Since nDPI relies on advanced techniques that go beyond simple port-based classification, these flows were not classified as SSH (for TCP port 22), Web (for TCP port 80) or Secure web traffic (for TCP port 443).

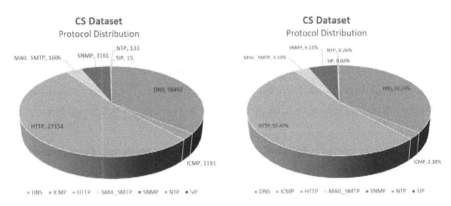

Figure 0.2: Ground truth results generated by nDPI (a) Number of Flows; (B) Percentage of Flows

As shown in this section, complete Ground Truth results were obtained by analyzing the payload in the traffic captures. However, with blind classification methods, various traffic properties should be extracted to be used as the classifier's input, which constitutes the next step.

1.2 Classifier Data (Traffic Parametrization)

After complete Ground Truth results were obtained, a parametrization of the flows existing in the data is made (Figure 4.2) in order to represent each of them as a vector or set of numerical properties. The resulting data will be the input for each of the blind classifiers, KNN based in our case.

As mentioned previously, existing blind classification methods in the literature consider a wide range of parameters from each of the elements to be classified. Consequently, using a custom nDPI tool, we extracted all the parameters that are potentially useful for blind classification as to have a large enough pool of traffic properties for subsequent experiments. Particularly, we considered all those parameters described in the literature (Moore, 2000) and a few additional ones related to higher order statistics. The complete set of considered parameters is listed in Annex-II, which includes around 60 variables of different natures. Annex-II shows the exhaustive list of all extracted parameters.

The values considered in the parameters vector include both basic and advanced statistical measures and flow properties. Two directions are considered for most parameters: UP, for the packets traveling from the lowest IP to the upper IP (when representing IP addresses as integers), and DOWN for the opposite direction. Among the parameters are also the usual ones included in most NetFlow-like flow analysis as average packet size, flow duration and the number of packets (Moore, 2000) while at the same time a more detailed description at temporary and signaling levels (e.g. inter-arrival times and the number of URG packets) is included.

As shown in Annex-II, the values for the parameters are obtained from the list of packets in a flow by analyzing just their sizes, timestamps, TCP flags, if any, and the direction of the packets. This way, no inspection of the payload beyond TCP/UDP headers is made, thus preserving the privacy of the users at the application layer.

The parametrization of all the flows in the captured datasets was made through a tool specially pre-developed for this purpose.

It is important to note that, for the classification scenarios addressed in this journal, not all of these parameters are used. In fact, at the parametrization phase, it was too early to determine, a priori, which traffic parameters are going to be used specifically. This had to be answered in regard to the research and experimental progress.

1.3 Evaluation Method

Once the experimental setup to evaluate and compare classification methods is complete, evaluation metrics should be defined and selected from those described and used in the literature.

An evaluation metric is used to quantify the classification capabilities of a given method, being used as the main indicators for the choice of one classification method over the other. The most intuitive composite metric is the Percent Correct (P_C), which accounts for the total number of elements correctly classified, N_c, related to the total number of elements to classify, N, as shown in the below equation:

Equation 0.1: Percentage Correct

$$P_C = \frac{N_C}{N}$$

Unfortunately, in imbalanced datasets, as is the case with the captured traffic, this measure is meaningless. Therefore, other metrics are required to assess classifiers performance when imbalanced datasets are present.

In the literature, basic per class and composed evaluation metrics can be found in the context of traffic classification although most of them are also useful in other applications. For simplicity reasons, these metrics are explained next for a binary classification scenario (two classes, A and B), although the same ones can be used for multi-class classification scenarios.

Four possible situations can be identified, considering class A:

- **True Positive (TP)**:

An element in class A is correctly classified as belonging to A,

- **False Positive (FP)**:

An element in class B is incorrectly classified as belonging to B,

- **True Negative (TN)**:

An element in class B is correctly labeled as class B,

- **False Negative (FN)**:

An element in class A is incorrectly labeled as class B.

Ideally, classifiers should maximize, per class, T_P and T_N while minimizing F_N and F_P. However, more complex metrics are needed to evaluate these evaluation parameters in relation to each other. Examples of composed evaluation metrics include precision or accuracy, completeness, correctness, and sensitivity or recall.

Most of the existing works in the literature consider complex evaluation parameter like the classification accuracy as the main evaluation metric. In this work, and as we aim to address

KNN dataset deficiencies part of which is the class imbalance problem, we focus on per class evaluation parameter (Tp) rather on generic classification evaluation parameter like Pc. Tp rate evaluation parameter calculates the relevance per class and we are addressing this problem when the dataset deficiency exists.

Alternatively, a confusion matrix is able to illustrate the classifier performance on a per class basis. It shows the number of instances recognized by the classifier for each class, given the actual class. Table 3 shows an example of a confusion matrix for the binary classes scenario (A and B), where N_{ij} denotes the number of instances with actual class i classified as j. The diagonal of this matrix represent the correct decisions for each class. Values outside the diagonal represent the number of classification errors, which should be minimized.

Classified / Actual	A	B
A	N_{aa}	N_{ab}
B	N_{ba}	N_{bb}

Table 0.1: Confusion matrix for multi-classification scenario (classes A, B and C)

Particularly, we focus on the flow rather than packet Tp as we consider that classifying flows is semantically more significant and more adequate to most traffic engineering tasks than classifying packets (too fine-grained level) or host-community (too coarse-grained level).

1.4 The Classification Software

To generate evaluation parameters for blind KNN classifiers, we use Weka (waikato, 2019) which is an open source machine learning tool. Weka is a java based program built on object-oriented bases that support clustering, classification, feature selection, and data visualization. Weka (waikato, 2019) contains a wide set of algorithms implemented in its source code.

Weka has a graphical user interface that allows the user to run any of the above data science actions, and it could be imported as a library for the purpose of adding a new algorithm. Weka users have the option to customize the graphical version by adding new custom algorithms. It supports multiple data containers (sql database, csv, arff files) that can feed the classifier's input.

In our implementation, we used arff input formats converted from CSV, we also customized both the Weka GUI interface, to simplify and visualize classification testing, together with the CLI version of Weka.

For creating new classifier classes from the source code, we had to use a helper program, Ant (apache, apache, 2019) , which is used to compile and build separate classes into one jar file. By editing Weka source code, one can add new or customized algorithms both to the CLI and to the graphical user interface.

1.5 The Classification Hardware

Classification programs were compiled with GCC v4.4.3 with -O3 optimization level. The server's hardware specifications include 8 GB of memory, 2 Intel(R) Xeon(R) 2.66 GHz processors with 4 cores each.

Chapter 5. Experimental Results

In this chapter, we describe the experiments done to firstly assess KNN in computer traffic classification context, using the experimental setup described in chapter 4, then to evaluate the proposed classifier CWKNN and compare it with existing approaches.

For this purpose, we start first by running the default Ibk classifier (KNN classifier in Weka) over the features vector presented previously, as extracted from the CS dataset. We address KNN classification parameters, as mentioned in Chapter 4, starting with the K value, distance type and classification parameters or attributes (also named features vector).

1.1. Selecting KNN K value, Distance Type and Traffic Attributes

1.1.1 Selecting the Distance Type

Regarding the distance type, we used the Euclidean distance (Equation 1). Our experiments show that the same classification accuracy, expressed in T_P can be obtained when switching between Manhattan, Minkowski or Euclidean distances, as shown in the below Figure:

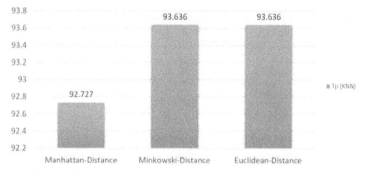

Figure 1.1.1: KNN Classification results (in TP) for the same dataset but for different distance types

As shown in Figure 5.1, for our experimental testbed and dataset, both Malinowski and Euclidean distances slightly outperform Manhattan while giving the same classification results. For this reason, we choose to proceed with the rest of our experiments using the Euclidean distance type.

1.1.2 Selecting Discriminative Attributes

We also ran the default feature selection algorithm, applied to KNN, in order to decrease the problem dimensionality. We choose the default "Attribute Selector" algorithm in Weka that evaluates the worth of each attribute by measuring the impact of leaving it out from the full set instead of considering its worth in isolation.

Our results show that to maintain a minimum to 89.35% of overall T_P average for all classes in the dataset, compared to 98.5% when all attributes (complete list in Annex-II) are applicable in the input feature vector, the below attributes should be present:

Selected Attributes	Description
PORT 1	Port associated to lower IP (IP LOW)
NPACKETS UP	UP Number of packets in the flow (UP Direction)
NPACKETS DOWN	Number of packets in the flow (DOWN Direction)
PACKETS SIZE UP	Total size of the exchanged packets (UP Direction)
PACKETS SIZE DOWN	Total size of the exchanged packets (DOWN Direction)
PAYLOAD SIZE	Total size of payloads in exchanged packets
PAYLOAD SIZE UP	Total size of payloads in exchanged packets (UP Direction)
PAYLOAD SIZE DOWN	Total size of payloads in exchanged packets (DOWN Direction)
DURATION	Duration of the flow (in microseconds)

Table 1.1.1: Minimum Set of Selected Attributes for maintaining 89.35% of Tp with KNN, for K=3

This means that amongst the 59 attributes or parameters extracted in section 4, the aforementioned attributes are the most discriminative due to having the highest. This is not to say that the remaining attributes are useless, but at least, for KNN and the testbed we prepared, the aforementioned attributes are the highest contributors. Eventually, for another algorithm, even for another set of protocols, remaining attributes can show higher contribution rates.

Moreover, it is noticeable here that the volume of exchange in both directions of the traffic is discriminative for the classification decision, which is an intrinsic feature for each application type. For instance, interactive traffic like SIP can be symmetrical in terms of volume of exchange while this is not the case for MAIL_SMTP or for FTP protocols. Another remarkable result with the selected features is that port numbers (TCP or UDP) are still contributing in the classification, but they are not the only contributor. As shown through our experiments, port numbers are no longer the main discriminative value with ML based blind classification methods (KNN in our case), when compared to IANA port-based classification (waikato, 2019) .

1.1.3 Selecting K value

We ran several experiments when varying the value of K, while fixing the previous parameters (Euclidean distance, while using all traffic attributes). Figure 5.2 shows the results of T_P value averaged on all application classes existing in the CS dataset for different values of K.

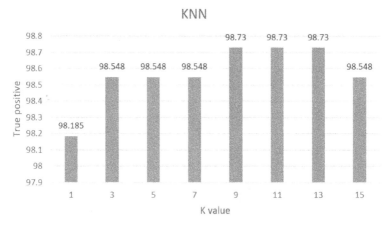

Figure 1.1.2: True positive values for the native KNN classifier, for different values of K

As shown in Figure 5.2, the T_P is the same for a few values of K (e.g. for K= 3, 5 and 7). From a classification standpoint, K=3 leads to the same result as K=7, at least for the dataset we have. Moreover, no more than 0.2% increase in the T_P can be noticed when the value nearest neighbors is increased to K=9, at the cost of increased computational cost, as compared to K=3. As a result, for the dataset we have, the optimal value of K to be used is K=3, both from a classification accuracy and computational cost standpoints.

1.2. Comparison with KNN and WKS

1.2.1 Overall Results

After implementing CWKNN as described in the previous section, we apply it, together with KNN and WKS on the CS dataset for various values of K (3 through 7) and using Euclidean distance. The below Figure summarizes the results we obtained

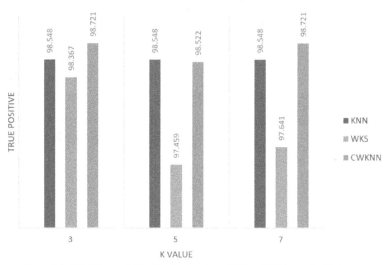

Figure 0.1: WCKNN overall Classification Results vs. KNN and WKS, over the CS dataset

Figure 5.3 shows the overall classification results expressed in T_p and averaged for all protocols existing in the CS dataset. As it can be clearly seen in Figure 5.3, the WKS algorithm is not able to provide any remarkable enhancement over the native KNN. On the other hand, CWKNN is outperforming both KNN and WKS algorithms. CWKNN is steadily giving the same or better classification results for different values of K. Although the enhancement is slight (0.2% to 1%), but this related to the CS dataset, especially for the training samples distribution and class intersections which affect the weight for each class.

To validate the obtained results, we used external datasets, namely DS1 and DS2 from Weka (waikato, 2019) and applied all the three algorithms to obtain the results shown in Figure 5.4.

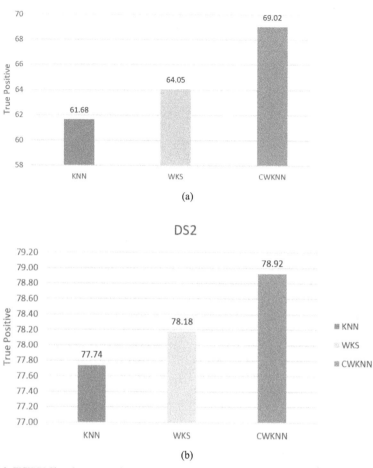

Figure 0.2: WCKNN Classification Results, compared to KNN, WKS, for k=3 over two external datasets: (a) DS1; (b) DS2

Similarly to Figure 5.3, Figure 5.4 shows the overall classification results expressed in T_p and averaged for all protocols existing in the DS1 and DS2 datasets. Again, CWKNN was able to outperform both algorithms and this time with greater enhancement (around 7% T_p over KNN and 5% over WKS in Figure 5.4 (a) for DS1). The enhancement is proven to be thus dataset dependent since the proposed weighting mechanism is strongly related to the training samples distribution. However, CWKNN has not shown any degradation in the classification results when compared to KNN and WKS, for any of the datasets we tested.

1.2.2 Per Protocol Results

To get further insights on the behavior of KNN when individual classes are weighted, we extracted per class or protocol results, as can be summarized for selective protocols in the below Figure:

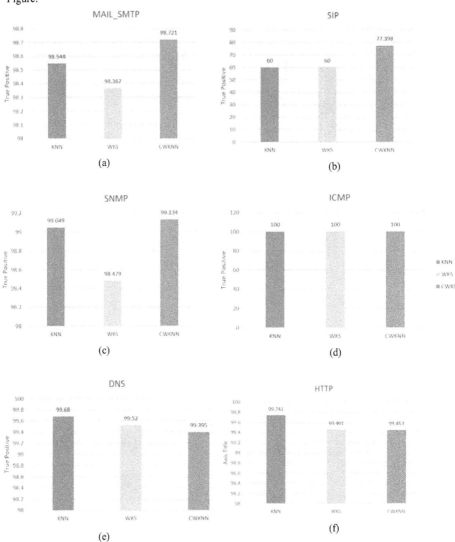

Figure 5.5: WCKNN Classification Results per protocol,compared to KNN,WKS,for k=3

As it can be seen in Figure 5.5, CWKNN is outperforming KNN and WKS for most of the individual protocols found in the CS dataset, in Figure 5.5 (a) Mail-SMTP, (b) SIP, (c) SNMP, or at least is giving the same or equal classification results, as is the case for the ICMP protocol in Figure (d). However, and for some protocols like DNS in Figure 5.5 (e) and HTTP (f), the T_p value was slightly decreasing (with less than 0.3%) when compared to KNN or WKS. This can be explained through the way classes are weighted as described in section 6. It seems that for these classes (DNS and HTTP), clusters were intersecting with other classes' clusters and they were assigned lower weights. This is not surprising since DNS and HTTP, as per the classical Internet user behavior, are the most two predominant protocols. As described earlier, the imbalance is an implication for clusters' intersections and lowering, therefore, the corresponding class weight. This does not mean, however, that CWKNN is not convenient for DNS and HTTP, but that it is slightly decreasing their classification results (due to being both imbalanced with intersected clusters) at the cost of increasing it for other protocols found in the CS dataset. However, this assumption needs further testing.

Chapter 6: Conclusions

1.1. Overview of the technique

In this work, we have explored and measured a new deficiency, related to KNN training samples distribution in the n-dimensional space and classes' intersections. We weighted classes accordingly in the training set. Then, we suggested class weighting scheme, then we derived a newly proposed Class Weight based KNN Classifier (CWKNN), an enhanced KNN algorithm that can account for sample distributions or classes intersections in KNN training sets.

Furthermore, we have assessed KNN algorithm in traffic classification contexts through an experimental test-bed that we build for this purpose.

1.2. Hypothesis

Our tests on real captured and Internet-based datasets showed up top 7% enhancements in the classification results, compared to the native and samples' weighted KNN approaches.

Moreover, and as per our testbed, we showed that K=3 and Euclidean distance type can lead to more than 98% of overall T_p in computer traffic classification context.

1.3. Advantages of Weighting Classes

Other than the classification results enhancement, CWKNN approach has many advantages including measuring training set validity and claiming some protocol(s) convenience for KNN.

In fact, assigning a weight for each class in KNN training set is new and advantageous compared to traditional KNN approaches like native or WKS based KNN. The below can be summarized as advantages for weighting classes through the CWKNN classification method:

✓ **Classification Accuracy:**
o Classification with CWKNN provides overall enhancements ranging from 0.2% to 7% in some cases over traditional KNN or weighted KNN samples methods.
o Classification with CWKNN is steadily enhanced for most protocols, while for others it shows the same or slightly decreased results (not more than 0.3%) for a few predominant or intersecting clusters classes.

30

✓ **Dataset Validity:**

CWKNN provides a dataset-dependent weight mechanism, thus, class weights for a given dataset can be used as an indicator of its validity for KNN training. This is new and important in the sense that network administrators and data scientists can evaluate the credibility of one dataset over the other when it concerns KNN based classifiers' training.

✓ **Protocol Convenience for KNN:**

For protocols which prove to hold statistically low class weights across several tested datasets (e.g. DNS and HTTP over the CS dataset), CWKNN can prove that these protocols are intrinsically inconvenient for KNN classification or may influence the classification of others when found in the training sets, even if with balanced number of samples. For such protocols, other classification algorithms should be used. However, this assumption needs further testing.

✓ **Weight Generalization:**

CWKNN class weighting mechanism can be generalized to cover any aspect related to class deficiencies in the KNN training sets like the imbalance or outliers problems. For instance, to address class imbalance problem, the same class weight we used in this work can be increased or decreased according to the deviation of the number of samples for each class from the overall average number of samples per class in the training set.

✓ **Intact Training Set:**

Compared to the process of dataset sampling used to solve the class imbalance problem, CWKNN does not manipulate training datasets, often captured from real working environments. Since it does not require sampling, instead, it decreases the weight for a class where sampling is required keeping the training set thus intact.

✓ **Independency from K value:**

One remarkable implication for the afore-mentioned near-ideal distribution described in chapter 3 is that KNN classification accuracy will be more independent of the value of K. When using CWKNN, the classification can become independent from K value when considering the distribution of the near-ideal sample in the training set, as previously described in the work. In fact, punishing intersecting classes is equivalent to approaching the near-ideal distribution, which as stated earlier will increase the level of independence from K value since most of the surrounding neighbors will have the same class. Independence from K value implies that computational gain is an eventual advantage of CWKNN, however, this assumption needs further testing.

1.4. Limitations

In this subsection, we present some considerations relevant to the ideal and near-ideal KNN training Set distribution and CWKNN approach presented throughout this work:

- **Dataset Dependency:** The main limitation is that results for each traffic class or application need to be dataset independent. However, this need to benchmark several real captured traffic sets in computer networks as to obtain near general average class weight that can be dataset independent. In the case two or more classes prove to be intersecting across several datasets, then, KNN should be deemed as inconvenient algorithm for these classes where another algorithm should be tested and the presence of such classes, as stated previously, may affect the influence of others even of the training set is balanced.

- **Cluster Shape:** The assumption of spherical shapes for each class cluster may not exactly reflect real world datasets where clusters' shapes may usually take irregular forms. However, for simplicity reasons, spherical forms were used to represent class clusters. Moreover, the way the radius is statistically derived from the training samples is supposed to minimize the differences in the n-dimensional space between the cluster actual shape and the spherical assumption considered in this work. An alternative to this could consist of considering advanced clustering techniques instead of the simple spherical representation of each cluster. However, this may result in more than one cluster for the same class and implies complicates the way to measure clusters' intersections which is less obvious for irregular cluster shapes.

- **Training vs. Testing Points Distribution:** Another consideration relates to the distinction the assumption for ideal KNN training points' distribution described previously and testing points' distribution in the n-dimensional space which should not mixed up. Otherwise, this could be regarded as limitation for our approach if not well elaborated.

Having an ideal training set distribution does not imply any condition or assumption on the testing points' distribution. In fact, compared to other machine learning approaches, the strength of KNN appears the most in cases where intersections between classes in the n-dimensional do exist. Therefore, what we attempt here is to adjust KNN decision according to training points' deviation from the distribution we believe as ideal. Measuring this deviation and considering it quantitatively in KNN classification decision (e.g. through weighting) is supposed, as discussed, to increase the overall reliability and accuracy of KNN classification. As such, we do not consider or imply any assumption on the testing points' distribution in the n-dimensional space. Nevertheless, testing points' distribution will surely affect the overall KNN accuracy: if most of the testing points fall inside disjoint clusters, the "idealism" of the

KNN training set will have greater impact on the overall reliability of KNN classification, otherwise, it will be of less importance since most of KNN decisions will be controversial due to testing points falling in intersected or empty zones.

- **Associated Computational Cost:** computational cost differences between default and CWKNN should be considered.

1.5. Future Work

Our weighting approach can be easily generalized to cover other aspects of the data set deficiencies related to the characteristics of the classes inside KNN training sets.

To extend this work, future experiments can be dedicated to generalize the class weight formula as to include class imbalance problem and any other unexplored class deficiencies. One can also consider advanced clustering techniques instead of the simple spherical representation with the adaptation of a more complex scheme to measure clusters' intersections.

The computational gain that can be obtained with CWKNN can also take research attention, especially that our approach is promising for being independent of the value of K, the nearest neighbor's number. Furthermore, a benchmark using CWKNN can be used to discover which network protocol(s) can be steadily affected lower weights than others to claim their inconvenience for KNN classifiers or influence on the classification accuracy of others.

In addition to that we tend to add other evaluation parameters such as precision and recall.

References

Alok Tongaonkarⱪ, R. T. (2014). Towards self adaptive network traffic classification.

apache. (2019). *apache*. Retrieved from apache: https: //ant.apache.org/

apache. (2019). *ntop*. Retrieved from ntop: https: //www.ntop.org/products/deep-packet-inspection/ndpi/

contributors, W. (2020, 11 30). *Mahalanobis distance*. Retrieved from Wikipedia, The Free Encyclopedia: https://en.wikipedia.org/wiki/Mahalanobis_distance

digitalguardian. (2019). *digitalguardian*. (digitalguardian) Retrieved from digitalguardian: https: //digitalguardian.com/blog/what-deep-packet-inspection-how-it-works-use-cases-dpi-and-more

Hou Kaihu, Z. H. (2018). A Weighted KNN Algorithm Based on Entropy.

IANA. (2013). *IANA Port Numbers*. Retrieved 01 2013, from IANA : http: //www.iana.org/assignments/ port-numbers

J. Khalife, J. V. (2013). *On the Performance of OpenDPI in Identifying P2P Truncated traffic* (Vols. VOL. 8, NO. 1). JOURNAL OF NETWORKS.

J. Khalife, J. V. (2014). A multilevel taxonomy and requirements for an optimal traffic-classification model. *24*(2).

Jigang Wang, P. N. (2006). Improving nearest neighbor rule with a simple adaptive Distance measure. *International Conference on Natural Computation*. ICNC 2006: Advances in Natural Computation.

Kumar, N. S. (2018). An Enhancement of k-Nearest Neighbor Classification Using Genetic Algorithm.

Lei Dinga, J. L. (n.d.). Internet Traffic Classification Based on Expanding Vector of Flow.

Liu W., C. S. (2011). Class Confidence Weighted kNN Algorithms for Imbalanced Data Sets. *Huang J.Z., Cao L., Srivastava J. (eds) Advances in Knowledge Discovery and Data Mining. vol 6635*. Berlin, Heidelberg: Springer.

machinelearningmastery. (2018). *machinelearningmastery*. (machinelearningmastery) Retrieved from machinelearningmastery: https: //machinelearningmastery.com/classification-versus-regression-in-machine-learning/

Min Zhang, M. Q. (2017). New Classification Algorithm WKS Based on Weight. *2017 IEEE 19th International Conference on e-Health Networking, Applications and Services (Healthcom)*. Dalian, China: IEEE.

Moore, A. D. (2000). *Discriminators for use in Flow-based Classification. Tech. rep*. Retrieved from http://www .eecs.qmul.ac.uk/ tech_ reports/RR-05-13.pdf.

pseudo_teetotaler. (2019). *stack overflow*. Retrieved from stack overflow: https: //stackoverflow.com/questions/33884325/ideal-k-value-in-KNN-for-classification

Shweta Taneja, C. G. (2014). Enhanced K-Nearest Neighbor Algorithm Using Information Gain and Clustering. *2014 Fourth International Conference on Advanced Computing & Communication Technologies.* IEEE.

TM, M. (2018). Pulsar Selection Using Fuzzy knn Classifier. *Future Computing and Informatics Journal (2018).* IEEE.

waikato. (2019). *waikato.* (waikato.ac.) Retrieved from waikato: https: //www.cs.waikato.ac.nz/ml/weka/

whuber. (2020, 11 06). *stackexchange.com.* Retrieved from https://stats.stackexchange.com/questions/62092/bottom-to-top-explanation-of-the-mahalanobis-distance

Zhang, S. (2019). Cost-Sensitive KNN Classification.

Appendix I: KNN pseudocode

```
Start
INPUT(X,Y,x,K)// X is a collection of labeled instances, each with
a number of Attributes
X1{A1,A2,...,An}

// Y  is a Set of all class labels for X
Y:{y1,y2,...,ym}
// x:unknown instance, K: number of voting neighbors, y is the
class of x

Function CalculteDistance:
      Pass In:
X,Y,x,K
      FOR every instance in X:
            init total  = 0
            FOR every attribute of instance:
                  total=total + distance(A instance, A x)
            Pass out:
            instance, total
            END FOR
            store (K instances closest to x)
      ENDFOR
      Pass Out:
      stored instances
END Function

Function Classify
      Pass In: stored instances
      FOR  every instance in stored_instances:
            get class
            count occurrences of each class
            y = majority class occurrences in K nearest neighbors.
```

```
        ENDFOR
        Pass Out: y
END Function


call CalculteDistance
call classify
END
```

Appendix II: Traffic Parameters

Name	Type	Description
		Identification set
FLOW ID	ui32	Number of the flow (in the file)
ID PROT	ui32	Protocol as identified by dpi flow
IP LOW	ui32	Minor IP address in the session tuple
IP UPPER	ui32	Greater IP address in the session tuple
PORT1	ui16	Port associated to lower IP (IP LOW)
PORT2	ui16	Port associated to upper IP (IP UPPER)
PROT	ui8	Transport protocol (TCP/UDP or as in header: 6/17)
DIR	ui8	Direction of the first observed packet (0 or UP if IP LOW- (IP UPPER 1 or DOWN otherwise)
FIRST TIME	ui64	Timestamp for the first observed packet (microseconds)
LAST TIME	ui64	Timestamp for the last observed packet (microseconds)
		Basic data and statistics (Netflow like
NPACKETS	ui64	Number of packets in the flow
NPACKETS UP	ui64	Idem UP direction
NPACKETS DOWN	ui64	Idem DOWN direction
PACKETS SIZE	u16	Total size of the exchanged packets
PACKETS SIZE UP	u16	Idem UP
PACKETS SIZE DOWN	u16	Idem DOWN
PAYLOAD SIZE	u16	Total size of payloads in exchanged packets
PAYLOAD SIZE UP	u16	Idem UP
PAYLOAD SIZE DOWN	u16	Idem DOWN
DURATION	u64	Duration of the flow (in microseconds)
MEAN PACKETS SIZE	float	Mean size of the packets in the flow
Name	Type	Description
MEAN PACKETS SIZE UP	float	Idem UP
MEAN PACKETS SIZE DOWN	float	Idem DOWN
MEAN INTERARRIVAL	float	Mean time among consecutive packets in flow
MEAN INTERARRIVAL UP	float	Idem only for UP packets
MEAN INTERARRIVAL DOWN	float	Idem only for DOWN packets
N SIGNALING	u16	Number of packets with flags
N SIGNALING UP	u16	Idem UP

N SIGNALING DOWN	u16	Idem DOWN
SHORT PACKETS	u64	Number of short packets in flow (Default: < 100 packets)
SHORT PACKETS UP	u64	Idem UP
SHORT PACKETS DOWN	u64	Idem DOWN
LONG PACKETS	u64	Number of long packets in flow (Default: ¿= 100 packets)
LONG PACKETS UP	u64	Idem UP
LONG PACKETS DOWN	u64	Idem DOWN
MAX INTERARRIVAL	u64	Maximum time among consecutive packets in flow
MAX INTERARRIVAL UP	u64	Idem only for UP packets
MAX INTERARRIVAL DOWN	u64	Idem only for DOWN packets
MIN INTERARRIVAL	u64	Minimum time among consecutive packets in flow
MIN INTERARRIVAL UP	u64	Idem only for UP packets
MIN INTERARRIVAL DOWN	u64	Idem only for DOWN packets
MAXLEN	u16	Maximum packet size
MAXLEN UP	u16	Idem UP
MAXLEN DOWN	u16	Idem DOWN
MINLEN	u16	Minimum packet size
MINLEN UP	u16	Idem UP
MINLEN DOWN	u16	Idem DOWN
NACKS	u64	Number of packets with ACK flag active
NFIN	u64	Idem FIN
NSYN	u64	Idem SYN
NRST	u64	Idem RST
NPUSH	u64	Idem PSH
NURG	u64	Idem URG
NECE	u64	Idem ECE
NCWD	u64	Idem CWD
NACK UP	u64	Number of packets with ACK flag (only UP)
NACK DOWN	u64	Idem DOWN
NFIN UP	u64	Idem FIN and UP
NFIN DOWN	u64	Idem FIN and DOWN
NRST UP	u64	Idem RST and UP
NRST DOWN	u64	Idem RST and DOWN

Appendix III: WCKNN pseudo-code

```
Start
INPUT(X,Y,x,K)// X is a collection of labeled instances, each with
n number of Attributes
X1{A1,A2,...,An}

// Y  is a Set of all class labels for X
Y:{y1,y2,...,ym}

// x:unknown instance, K: number of voting neighbors, y is the class
of x

//C is a set of instances corresponding for the centroid of each
class
C:{c1,c2,...,cm}

//SDI set of instances contains the standard deviation of each
attribute per class
SDI{   [y1(sdv_attribute1,   sdv_attribute2,   sdv_attribute   n)]
[y2(sdv_attribute1,   sdv_attribute2,   sdv_attribute   n)],…,
[ym(sdv_attribute1, sdv_attribute2, sdv_attribute n)]

//R is a set of radiuses for all classes
R{r_y1,r_y2,…,r_ym)
//Com set of combination of two classes
Com{[y1,y2],…,[ym-1,ym]}

//W set of weights per classes
W{w1,w2,wm}

Function CalculateCentroid
Pass IN:
X
```

```
INIT instances C
FOR Every instance in X:
        FOR Every attribute in instance of each class:
                count occurrences of each Y
                calculate sum attribute
        END FOR
END FOR

FOR Every class in Y:
init instance c
        FOR Every attribute in X:
                init center_att = 0
                center_att = divide sum attributes over number of
occurrences of corresponding class
                If attribute position == C attribute position:
Store value of center_att  In C
                END IF
        ENDFOR
ADD  instance c to instances C
ENDFOR
Pass Out:
C
END Function

Function calculte_standard_deviation:
Pass IN:
X, C, occurrence of each class
init instances SDI
FOR EVERY attribute in A:
        init total =0
        FOR EVERY CLASS IN Y:
init instance_SDV
                total = 0
                init difference 0
                FOR Every instance in X:
```

```
                    IF Y(instance)  = CLASS
                        difference = attribute of  instance -
attribute of C
                        difference =  difference * difference
                  END IF
            ENDFOR
            total  = SQRT(difference /  occurrence of class)


 if  (attribute  position  (attribute)  ==  attribute  position
(instance_sdv)  and class(attribute) == class (instance_sdv ) :
 attribute_value (instance_sdv) = total
END IF
END FOR //class
ADD instance_sdv to SDI
END FOR //attribute
Pass Out:
SDI
End Function


Function calculate_radius
Pass IN:
SDI
FOR EACH instance in SDI:
      Init total = 0
      FOR EACH attribute in instance:
```

$$Total = \sum_1^{SDI\ classes\ number} attribute\_value(attribute)^2$$

```
PASS OUT:
R
END Function


Function Intersections:
Pass IN:
Com, R, C
FOR EACH pair in Com:
      Init sum =0
```

42

```
        Init R1,R2
        R1 = radius y1 in pair
        R2  = radius y2 in pair
Calculate  distance centroid1 and  centroid2
        Sum = R1+R2
        IF Sum <= distance:
                Decrease weight of y1 and y2
        End IF
        Store weight1, weight2
        END Function
Function CalculteDistance:
        Pass In:
 X,Y,x,K,W
        FOR every instance in X:
                init total  = 0
                FOR every attribute of instance:
                        total=total +distance(A instance,A x)
                End for        // attribute
total =total/(1⁄w)
pass out:
instance, total
                END FOR
                store (K instances closest to x)
        ENDFOR
        Pass Out:
        stored instances
END Function

Function classify(storedInstances):
        Pass In: stored instances
        FOR  every instance in stored_instances:
                get y
                count occurrences of each Y
                y = label with highest occurrences
        ENDFOR
```

```
        Pass Out:
y
END Function
Call CalculateCentroid
call calculte_standard_deviation
call calculate_radius
call Intersectios
call calculteDistnace
call classify
END
```

Publisher: Eliva Press SRL

Email: info@elivapress.com

Eliva Press is an independent publishing house established for the publication and dissemination of academic works all over the world. Company provides high quality and professional service for all of our authors.

Our Services:
Free of charge, open-minded, eco-friendly, innovational.

-Free standard publishing services (manuscript review, step-by-step book preparation, publication, distribution, and marketing).
-No financial risk. The author is not obliged to pay any hidden fees for publication.
-Editors. Dedicated editors will assist step by step through the projects.
-Money paid to the author for every book sold. Up to 50% royalties guaranteed.
-ISBN (International Standard Book Number). We assign a unique ISBN to every Eliva Press book.
-Digital archive storage. Books will be available online for a long time. We don't need to have a stock of our titles. No unsold copies. Eliva Press uses environment friendly print on demand technology that limits the needs of publishing business. We care about environment and share these principles with our customers.
-Cover design. Cover art is designed by a professional designer.
-Worldwide distribution. We continue expanding our distribution channels to make sure that all readers have access to our books.

www.elivapress.com

www.ingramcontent.com/pod-product-compliance
Lightning Source LLC
Chambersburg PA
CBHW070902070326
40690CB00009B/1961